Also by Rae Armantrout

Entanglements (2017)
Partly (2016)
Itself (2015)
Just Saying (2013)
Money Shot (2011)
Versed (2009)
Next Life (2007)
Collected Prose (2007)
Up to Speed (2004)
Veil: New and Selected Poems (2001)
The Pretext (2001)
True (1998)
Made to Seem (1995)
Necromance (1991)
Precedence (1985)
The Invention of Hunger (1979)
Extremities (1978)

Rae Armantrout

Wesleyan University Press
Middletown, Connecticut

Wesleyan Poetry Series

Wesleyan University Press
Middletown CT 06459
www.wesleyan.edu/wespress
2018 © Rae Armantrout
Manufactured in the United States of America
Designed by Mindy Basinger Hill
Typeset in Minion Pro

Library of Congress Cataloging-in-Publication Data

Names: Armantrout, Rae, 1947– author.

Title: Wobble / Rae Armantrout.

Description: Middletown, Connecticut : Wesleyan
University Press, [2018]

Series: Wesleyan poetry

Identifiers: LCCN 2018002974 (print) |
LCCN 2018005935 (ebook) | ISBN 9780819578242
(ebook) | ISBN 9780819578235 (cloth : alk. paper)

Classification: LCC PS3551.R455 (ebook) |
LCC PS3551.R455 A6 2018 (print) | DDC 811/.54—dc23

LC record available at https://lccn.loc.gov/2018002974

5   4   3   2

This project is supported in part by an award
from the National Endowment for the Arts.

Contents

Making   *1*

Asymmetries   *3*

Speech Acts   *4*

The Craft Talk   *5*

Conflation   *6*

Overtake   *8*

Audience   *9*

Background
Information   *11*

Wobble   *13*

Reception   *15*

My Pleasure   *17*

My Bad Self   *18*

You Know   *19*

Object
Permanence   *20*

Arch   *21*

Feeling Today   *23*

Boreal   *24*

Say   *25*

Regime Change   *26*

Credible   *28*

Return   *29*

Openings   *30*

Conjunctions   *31*

Incoming   *32*

Accomplices   *33*

Hoard   *35*

Hell   *36*

Silos   *37*

Trellis   *38*

The Emotional Life
of Plants   *39*

Those   *40*

Alone   *41*

Echoes   *42*

Thorned   *43*

Revisions   *44*

What's Coming   *46*

Tunnel Vision   *47*

Incorporation   *48*

The Third Person   *50*

Flicker   *51*

My Erasures   *53*

Rankings   *54*

Chronos   *55*

Old Woman's Lament
in Autumn   *56*

Sparks   *57*

To   *58*

Practicing   *59*

Are   *60*

Shapes   *62*

Object   *64*

Design Elements   *66*

Some Body   *67*

I and I   *69*

Household   *70*

Mother   *71*

Chord   *73*

Chimera   *74*

Near   *76*

Life History   *78*

A Few Questions   *79*

The Difference   *81*

Instruction   *82*

In the Future   *83*

The Trick   *84*

Accordingly   *85*

Moment to
Moment   *87*

Fusion   *88*

Seams 90

Nothing 91

Distinguish 92

Presents 93

Spun 95

Traffic 96

Negotiations 97

Refresh 99

Translations 100

Signaling 101

Bees 102

The Show 103

Vessels 104

The Act 106

Inner 108

Object Lessons 109

Normal 111

Hate 112

Ahead 113

Give Pause 115

Hence 117

Somewhere 118

Judgment 119

Logistics 120

Flux 122

Cottage Industry 124

Practice 125

Trance 126

It Is 127

So 128

∿

Acknowledgments 131

WOBBLE

Making

"What made this happen?"
you ask every time

as if
compulsion itself
were mandatory,

the way light travels
at the speed of light

"because it must"

~

It is in no sense
essential

that this crown of leaves,
sifted by wind

as if turning over
some problem,

is a gray-green
brightening into rust-red

at the tips

or that its equivocations
fill this instant

to the brim.

~

While light
has caught up

to itself
again

and only seems
to be making

time

Asymmetries

I'm thinking about you and you're humming while cutting a piece of wood.
I'm positive you aren't thinking about me which is fine as long as you
aren't thinking about yourself. I know and love the way you inhabit
this house and the occasions we mutually create. But I don't know
the man you picture when you see yourself walking around
the world inside your head and I'm jealous
of the attention you pay that person
whom I suspect
of being devious.

Speech Acts

Something's going around.
The crows

started it.
No language

can tell us
which crow.

~

You who
in the

mama turnpike
sexy tough shit

steady state

thought bubble song
churn

~

What's new? Presence
as fad.

Humans
photo-bomb the planet,

pop up everywhere
because incongruous

is funny

and we want you
to know

The Craft Talk

So that the best thing you could do, it seemed, was climb inside the machine that was language and feel what it wanted or was capable of doing at any point, steering only occasionally.

The best thing was to let language speak its piece while standing inside it— not like a knight in armor exactly, not like a mascot in a chicken suit.

The best thing was to create in the reader or listener an uncertainty as to where the voice she heard was coming from so as to frighten her a little.

Why should I want to frighten her?

Conflation

As a tree
is concerted

atmosphere. Each
one a certain

ambience

drawn in and held
until it turns

green?

~

You go on
drawing energy

from conflation, referring
to yourself

while implicating
other beings.

~

That's silly!

~

Silly tablecloth
of the nasturtium leaf,

flung out
on its too thin stem,

perfectly flat, in flight,
serene

Overtake

Thought catches up
to jotting. Pointless

to go on. Jotting
catches up to thought.

~

Dream I am pouring coffee beans, snap beans, and grains of sand from a
    packet
into a hotel coffee maker. I eat a snap bean while trying to figure out what
went wrong. When I fall back to sleep, the dream is there. I can't say it
    "continues."

~

He asks me to stay up, watch
the tsunami appear

above the swimming pool
again,

so wrong
people can only stare

Audience

1

Phlegmatic and unbending,

Russell Crowe as Noah

teaches us

to hold the door

against "the desperate"

and "the many"

threatened by catastrophic

climate change—

worse than we'd guessed

and more immediate.

2

Are we stowaways?

3

Zipper fracture

involves simultaneous

stimulation of parallel

horizontal wells.

Viscoelastic

surfactant gel

has/has not been

adequately described

Background Information

1

There's a lot going on in
"the"
zombie apocalypse.

But wouldn't she recognize
that her mother
was a zombie?

I mean zombies
are a thing.

2

The last thing she did
was point
to one corner of the ceiling

with a horrified stare.
The nurse called this "a seizure."

As if words
drained experience
of content and continued

to accumulate.

As if words
were sealed containers
stored for safekeeping.

3

The background
is everything

that, for now,
can be safely

ignored

Wobble

1

Imagine you're trying

to locate a lost

aircraft

by the way its pings

come in relation

to the wobble

of a satellite

beginning to lose

orbit—

and you feel

no fear.

2

Now the heavy cables
dip into layers
of blue
and lavender—

almost lackadaisical—
and at either end
emit

World's Smallest Pets,
BBQ Pit Wars

Reception

"No market left
emerging."

Capital's interior monologue
lines the jetway
at Kennedy

∿

By adjusting their orbits slightly,
electrons can reach out

and conjure

the tug
of more than one

nucleus.

∿

One man plays

"Somewhere Over the Rainbow"
and "Hernando's Hideaway"

on an accordion
in Spain.

∿

On a silent
American Airlines' screen

somewhere over the Atlantic
a woman cartwheels

toward Marriott
reception

above the words,
"Stay amazing!"

My Pleasure

Red brick pillars
prop the roof
of a corrugated tin shack.

~

It is my pleasure
and my privilege
not to understand this.

~

A swooping disc
of loud starlings
takes its evening spin
above the park.

~

Skinny horses
pulling carriages
bearing the logo
"Movistar."

~

It is from this distance
that the object
resolves
into an image.

My Bad Self

"Superior," as in
I feel superior

to the hunched,
hobbling woman

with the fixed smile
walking in front of me.

With the beatific,
mysterious smile—

intended to deflect pity?
It's not working!

And, what's worse,
it's not necessary.

My gaze hovers
then rebounds,

spiteful as Tinkerbell
always.

You Know

You come in here
all high-heeled, prune-lipped,
tired.

~

You come in
marbled

with bullet-point
cirrus

as if the sky

~

You know the type.
White (speckled)

mantis
that mimes an orchid

like his mother dressed him.

All dead-eye

Object Permanence

What if the ability
to capture
emblems in the wild
won't validate us?

What if displaying
our embarrassing flaws
won't save us—

say being dead
but kittenish?

～

I can't show you anything
new, not even

an empty room
behind a velvet rope.

Least of all that!

There's a Lexus
spinning in a parking lot

because a mountain road is
"so cliché."

It's throwing up dust, then more,
but you know the car's

still in there
somewhere,

still voguing

Arch

1

Like an arched eyebrow
traveling alone, you drift,

seahorse,

a forgotten, persistent
question.

Despite your skeptical
attitude, it's true

that your numbers are crashing.

Still, you are rumored
to consume

up to 3,000 baby
shrimp per day!

2

Who doesn't want
to be a revenant,

to go back to basics
in a big way

on the small screen
which, somehow, still

survives? "Terrific"
and "terrible"

are cousins after all.
Am I warm or cold?

I'm half-
rhyming, aiming right

between quick and dead
like we could

thread that needle
and keep going.

Feeling Today

Could it be
the problem of
modern reflexology
is to keep tongue in cheek
while cultivating
melancholy
in the red-shifted context
of the retro-surreal?

∿

Oh,
pale pink ballpoint
with ADVENTURE IMAGING
stamped on your carapace
in letters that mimic
a message
dug in wet sand
with a stick
by a castaway
on a soundstage
in the late
1950s,
you could almost
but not quite
mean what we
feel

Boreal

"Fairy dust," she said
and cried.

"Fairy dust" as if
for the night sky

to be green
phosphorescent sheets

was at last
what she needed

so that words
had meaning.

For this we shoved
a ball
back at mother,

for this ran off,
arms out,
across a field

Say

1

Says her Tarot reader says
she will soon have an experience
of nature
that will make her feel
more connected than ever.

2

Says blogs, Facebook,
and Instagram
have replaced poetry as ways
of taking
the private public.

3

Say the way the leaves
are black
and unbroken
on the light mesh
of that window screen

Regime Change

1

Equidistant
metal roses,

metal pinwheels,

metal faces
at the ends of
metal tongs

grimacing.

Look at all
the time
they had to mean!

2

Poets wanted
to bounce the leaves,

to burn the sun,

to modulate the day
as the engine noise
does not.

To replace the bird
and replace the bird again

in a new way.

3

There are things
you will be asked
to make note of.

You may be asked
whether a light
is brighter or dimmer
than before

Credible

Wrap the pine
in reflections,

points of light
on the glass balls
we hang up.

Now the night
is abuzz
with heralds,

shot through with
credible threats,

so many it seems
we must all be
sending them

so our cities
wink out
one by one

Return

1

Better to collect miniature trolls
beside toy bridges
and arrange them on doilies.

Best we commemorate old fears
until our heads are full

lest we trump up
some flesh and blood devil.

2

Someone's been walking
on your grave.

You have seen yourself
unexpectedly
in a mirrored door.

(though some have claimed
it's pleasant
to leave your body
then return)

Now you return
his gaze.

Openings

1

Because children suspect that objects conceal their powers and intentions,
animators make an alarm clock run, screaming, in circles.

2

Because as I lie facing the wall the bones of my eye socket hurt, I see myself
as an ancient skeleton recently unearthed. Then I appear in a reenactment
of the moments before my death, a clear-eyed young woman peering
from the mouth of a cave
into what I take to be
an open future.

Conjunctions

1

If
even pain
does not exist
except in
comparison,
then how far
down
does comparison go?

        Or what if
        pain
        and only pain
        can be
        alone?

2

The point
in the hawk's eye

and the forest
"taken as a whole"

are fine,
        inaccessible.

The problem
is in "or,"

in "and."

The problem is we're lost

Incoming

"Another year," I say
as if this were ironic.

～

Because it's now/
because I'm now

in two places
and thus not

myself,
I contain

the disturbance
of the incoming

pulse without

2

A stuffed tiger
upside down

in a cubicle
cubby

Accomplices

1

The one in which I laugh about my mismatched

shoes at the boarding gate and the one

in which I pass quietly through the apartments

of four strangers to reach the one

I'm subletting

are played out

"before my eyes" while being

narrated to an

accomplice.

Where is she

when I wake up?

2

All the souls

that swarmed

through me,

intense and complex,

as I first encouraged

then graded them,

have vanished.

Hoard

1

She went around preregistered
for her own eventual absence.

Not that she believed
her self-estrangement
would save her,
whatever that meant,

but she hoped
that registering this estrangement
with the proper authorities
might still

2

Nice as it was, she resented it—
this memory—this
riverboat hotel deck chair
in—Phoenix (?).

There was no place for it
in her already crowded rooms.

She was no hoarder!

But the alternative
seemed even worse

Hell

"Able for the first time
to view
large bronze statues
of Dr. Seuss characters."

What if
the wish to be precise
survives
the world of objects?

Thumb and forefinger
meet again
as if
for the first time,

tugging once more
on "as if"

Silos

What if you tell me an interesting story, full of humor and disappointment, and, a few months later, I mention it, and you answer, "I never said that" or "It didn't happen that way"? What then?

Now we would expect the umpire to swoop in with the video playback, but, of course, there is no umpire here.

Perhaps we are our own worst witnesses.

Is this what's meant by "information silos"?

Trellis

Sex is porn
when it's over there
and flat.

Identity porn:
Debbie does categories.

I like mine tubular,
branched.

I prefer it
trellised,

small clotted
roses strung up
on iron bars
at the window,

their round heads
like children's
looking in,

inappropriate.

Likeness is to truth
as red is to what?

Scent of truth
splashed over sentences.

The Emotional Life of Plants

An exciton consists
of the escaped negative
(electron)
and the positive hole
it left behind.

This binary system
is unstable
and must be transported quickly
to the processing center
which, in practice, means
the exciton must be left
strictly alone
so that it travels
all ways at once
going nowhere
but also
going directly
to the factory floor.

Leaving aside the question
of what it means
for a positive hole
to be "left behind"
and also to travel
as half of a system,
this happens because nothing
can be still
and because, for the lonely,
direction is meaningless

Those

"It is extremely difficult to explain,"
says the astronomer,
"why the sky is not more
mottled,"

why the far sides
of the universe
are mirror images
of one another

(while we who're packed
meme to meme
are so often
out of sync)

∿

All those I reconstruct
so faithfully
in dreams

in order
to defend myself
to somebody

∿

Some claim space
grew exponentially
between them
without disturbing them
in the least

Alone

Because we ate, you thought,
we sinned and
we would die
like other creatures.

~

To arrive
at an idea
as if
at a town
with long established,
if obscure,
customs.

~

Pioneer Villa Diesel
stands alone

Echoes

1

In the parking garage I shout,
"Come here Rae's car"
as if in fun. We *know* this works
only for Jim's phone
in the commercial. Then I try
"Abandon all hope" because
I think you'll like
the echoes.

2

The homeless man living next door
under the viaduct,
among the concrete
orca fins of
the city art project
shouts a stream
of what sounds like words
though we don't catch
even one

Thorned

You tap yourself
sharply
every few seconds.

～

Leaves, light, as,
as, only, sequence.

～

Bet you can't
draw earth up
through your long,
thorned ankles.

～

If only still.
Still only if.

～

Which parts of you
will still
answer?

～

If being is eventual

～

"They still haven't told me
what they plan
to do about it."

Revisions

Round and almost
freestanding,

the contrived
water-bodies

of, say, peaches

were just what you'd come
to expect.

Had you heard the story?

～

Was the first bit
too cutesy?

Was the last gasp
too obvious

with its "dulcet,
dissolving chimes"

dissolving?

～

At the last minute

replaced
whatever was killing

the birds
with whatever

is killing
the bees.

What's Coming

Put your own stamp
on sentience.

Keep a small ache
as a familiar.

Think: warm
pebbles in the concrete

or

cold pulse
of ocean.

~

August: the orange
wrappers
of the Reese's Cups
already labeled,
"Pumpkin."

Tunnel Vision

All events
placed
in the future
are strange
because the future
is not a place.

~

You think
to have some place
to go.

~

How many scanners
between now
and home?

~

The recorded voice
saying, "Breathe.
Don't breathe."

You'll do as you're told.

~

You funnel

Incorporation

1

"Make me up," said nothing.

It had a certain shape
in mind,

a string
with a loose loop
on top

like a longhand letter
traced by a child.

~

"induces a host
to synthesize compounds

which are then assembled
which are then assembled

into the correct
structure"

~

Then, then, then, then,
the storyteller stutters.

2

I have the idea that
something comes next,

something in particular,
though I don't know what,

have faith
that the correct

shape
will induce me

to incorporate it.

The Third Person

1

Her attention didn't wander so much as it was repeatedly pulled out of the text she was reading as if by a voice or stare. She scanned the recesses of her awareness to locate the source. There was a faint burning sensation in the middle distance. Maybe she had to pee. But the imperative was premature. Whatever this was, it could still flicker out or show itself in an entirely new light. She tried to find her place again in the crowd of words. This would be different for the first person, she thought.

2

I'm anxious when you leave so I must love you. But I don't like the story you're telling the strangers around us—rising sea levels, hemorrhagic fevers. I've told it more than once myself. Connect the dots and watch the shape emerge. "Cut it out," I want to say, though I don't know what I mean by "it."

Flicker

1

When it was them, our parents, dying,
the way they tried to deny what was happening,

the way they were angry at the wrong things
seemed of a piece with the way they'd always
been wrong about us, we thought,

the way they were wrong about the world
which they saw only through the haze
of their own swath of the past

so that it seemed natural for us to scoff,
inwardly, even at their deaths—

but now it was one of us threatening
to get up and walk out of the hospital
on his withered legs, sheer sticks,

because it was killing him.

2

"Clouds of methane rise
from dumps" outside our city

as I drop a square of soft cheese
through a slot
into the bin marked
"landfill."

3

Of course
I feel bad
about feeling good
about feeling bad
about this—

but as time speeds up,
everything will flicker.

My Erasures

My erasures were featured.

~

I collected debris
to sell as crash art,

          crush porn.

~

"Say goodbye to Lonesome George,"
the last Galapagos tortoise.

~

I was a pushover
for the laws
of physics.

~

I pictured us as two seals
hauled out
on a sunny rock,

the roar around us
a matter of course

Rankings

Screw smug survivors
talking about us
as if we weren't quite

           here.

We never really loved them.

And screw time
which pancakes things
but also makes distinctions.

~

We have time
to watch versions
then parodies
and rank them,

to play
pin the tail
on the apocalypse

and define our terms:

to engulf
is to cover
or surround;

a gulf
is a chasm

Chronos

for Ish Klein

1

We grade stories
and we reconcile accounts.

By night we binge
on *The Walking Dead*.

2

"An actual electron
emits and swallows
its own photons
now and then."

3

Confusing exchange
with use-value
makes the word "own"
a hot mess.

4

When I'm alone
I pose

my question:

Why is one
constant

always squared?

Old Woman's Lament in Autumn
for WCW

Sorrow is my corner store
where jack-o'-lantern balloons
get high on the last helium.

The endcap is gold today
with numbered bags
of Werther's Originals.

No one is Werther.

Last night a newscaster
mentioned an "elderly victim."
Don't call me that.

I'm old
and obdurate.

Sparks

Sharp, green
flames of weeds
give off
occasional yellow
flowers.

~

Weeds aren't flames?

They're God's tongues—
translucent, invasive.

~

To flicker: to sink
down and spring up,

to thrust.

To be the air
and also be the sun.

To

Girl turned to a tree,
sure, or a vine
turned to a girl.

But what did you mean
by "girl"?

Such slender,
double-jointed

reaching?
Rapunzel

letting her hair down
this wall

upon wall,

articulate
with tiny flowers—

solicitations
never meant for you.

~

Carpenter bee's buzz,

as its feet
touch pollen,

a deep throb

Practicing

As the sun finds you,
upstanding,

knotted
at intervals,

gray-green

As you were, limbs
aloft and

eagerly splayed,
still practicing

the old faith
as I do—

these words,
pushed to the fore,

posing

Are

I want to go on forming
letters,

willing this
fluidity

as if I could
pilot a stream

as it freezes
into shapes.

～

Soft clouds advancing
from the west, their
fripperies,
vagaries.

～

Pair of mockingbirds
on a wire, seining
the neighborhood
for sounds.

～

Apart from "is" and "are,"
verbs act out

metaphorically

～

Pen stopped, tip to page
for an instant

as if purpose
was ribbed,

striated

～

And even *they*

Shapes

Lake's pocked face.
Lake's dimpled face.

Lake's steel-grid
of ripples,

brighter
in the far reaches.

~

(The living make much
of differences.)

~

But ripple after ripple,
peak behind peak—

what need
do these things fulfill?

~

Riding the updraft,
two pairs of gulls

arc like pendulums,
changing places.

~

One man says
of another,

"He has 37
of my bird

shapes."

Object

At a stately pace,
this clump
of bubbles
tours the perimeter
of the cup.

~

"Living systems
make the most
of a set of
imposed constraints."

~

As our hostage
situation guest
said earlier

~

Belief systems
are parodies.

~

Glass lampstand
in the shape
of a bong
at an upscale hotel
in Berkeley.

~

Objects
that self-identify
as fads

vs. those that won't.

~

Slender and blond,
the poplar
has wandered
into its present
form

Design Elements

Green faces
of the prickly pear

like oval hand mirrors
set at angles

(and, of course,
spotted with thorns).

Each face has a large
topknot—

a bud.

～

A few titular
poles or pikes,

some with froufrou
fronds on top

catching late sun.

～

I like it
when the clouds

are retro—

puffs and dashes
of Morse code.

God's faux messages,
all in fun.

Some Body

1

When I first lie down, trying to sleep, there's a lump of dread and hurt in my midsection. When did this thing form? Was it always there? I remember being young—that is, I remember places I lived and some of the things I did. I lived in an expensive, unheated apartment in San Francisco and sat around with my poet friends at readings and in bars. I had written maybe 20 poems. I thought I was near the center of something and could aim to embody it. That's enough to get a person going.

2

    Vines pegged to stakes:

    veins over bones,

    the beginning
    or end of

    somebody.

        ~

        Weed tops turned
        white frizz up,
        blow off, get
        carried away.

~

But the uncertainty
in her eyes,

the hesitant steps

as if she were making
some mistake

I and I

1

We pursued our son and competed
to amuse him, first with toys, then
with stories, as we had done with
our friends.

To him it seemed as if, though roped
together, we each struggled to stand
in front, waving at him with a free hand.
Alarmed, he stepped back.

2

Cut loose

almost ply

shining

aisles between

low isle

after isle

Household

The climbing rose,
dead on one side,

half-killed by summer's heat,
looks like a stroke victim,

though its remaining leaves
wag idly enough.

What can I say
to make things better?

Yellow "lamps"
instead of leaves?

Yellow lamps
and this stagnant haze.

Come home.
We'll watch the debate.

Mother

1

I want to get
to the managed care

evening,
where the future appears

to stream directly
into the past

with brief time-outs,
"nows,"

for setting preferences.

2

When wolves converge
on prisons,

when bats cover
solar panels

crashing power grids,

a safari guide,
a scientist
with a troubled past,
and a secret agent

must concentrate
to solve problems.

3

A chemical tracer sent;
a firing sequence

repeated
(or tap dance performed)

to bring back
pieces

of the past
in 3-D and color.

That is not my mother!

Chord

A minor chord
incorporates cry
and denial
and is thus complete.

～

The lasting tang
of lemon tea:

the point at which
persistence
becomes surprising.

～

And cold custard buildings
topped with globes,
spars, humans
so oddly solid
as to seem beautiful

Chimera

Neurons phase lock
to produce an executive

summary;

a throng of fish,
each one swerving
to avoid the rest

in perfect equanimity

Chimera 2

Okay, mind
is a mackerel
bait ball.

Bigger is better.

Except what?

Except we love color
which doesn't even exist!

It's something we invent
without trying,
though we do quibble about it

as we do about the lives
of celebrities we've never met.

Red's a slut
and purple is so self-absorbed,

so abstracted.

·Near

It's hopeless.

The aliens don't get
our humor.

How to wear
Duck Dynasty

as part
of a body

of knowledge.

~

In our world
the past's a joke

because we laugh at
what scares us,

those zombie decades
extant

with all feeling
sucked out of them.

Our unthinkable
thoughts

recorded
on their quaint devices.

The present exists
so long

as we wink
at its near

unthinkability.

Is it like that
where you are?

Life History

Clouds, conjoined
and tattered,

freely budding,

unbeholden,

contriving at nothing.

We've left them
far above.

We've dug in.

We've gone through channels.

And here he was
hurting men

instead of women,
though he'd put it

a different way
because substitution

is the real thing
so I want

to hurt *that.*

A Few Questions

Is it that a pocket
enjoys being filled

or that the folds
want to be pushed

aside
because they're tired

of touching
one another?

~

What if my sex
fantasies don't
involve me,

but rather
two strangers?

~

As I rock,
the dazzle

on the glass lid
splits, the top

half turns red
crested, then subsides

into itself
again.

(To make this happen
feels like happiness.)

~

When the disc dissolves,
have I solved
for x?

The Difference

You worry about the past;
I'll worry about the future.

~

Two calico opossums
mate, bite, screech
behind the gas grill.

You tell everyone about this:
premonition? confession?

~

I'd like to demonstrate
the way

I can split
any difference.

~

In dreams
I find the evidence and yell,

"What's this?"

Instruction

I'm holding a baby
who was born yesterday.

I may be her mother;
that part's unclear.

We've missed our connection
so we're on the shuttle.

I point to her mouth
and say, "Mouth, mouth."

She mouths it back;
she's so precocious!

Then she's unresponsive,
dead.

A man's voice says, "Never

confuse a journey
with a lesson."

Now you tell me!
Who is this?

I'm being shown
a big map

of London
with two tour bus routes

marked out:
one red, one blue

In the Future

1

The mentalist could tell precisely
what the scriptwriters were thinking.

Naturally,
he was a smart-ass because,
like us, he was in on
the con.

Conscious.

We make plans
and begin to guess

how far
the future will

resemble us.

2

It is now almost certain
that in the future
in another country
in a room I can't picture
we will wriggle and jump
guided by long disused
habit,
accompanied by strangers—
who knows how dangerous,
how amused

The Trick

My brain tricked me
into sleeping.

My body tricked me
into waking up.

"What do you do?"

I trick children
into writing down their thoughts.

~

Pre-owned, lightly
excoriated subject
position available.

~

You don't have it
unless you can get it

down
and outside in

some kind of
box.

Accordingly

1

The object is "vibrant," "withdrawn,"
and "incoherent."

A small range of times
coexist within the object

or, if the object is large,
it may extend through times

that are unwilling
to coexist.

In this sense, the object
hasn't been itself lately.

2

A human uses part
of herself to think
of the rest
of herself as existing

"now."

This is labor intensive.

3

The "fellows"
from the Rockefeller Center,
a villa on a hill in Italy,
go dancing at a lakefront hotel
to the sounds of a string trio
who play "Puttin' on the Ritz"
and "New York, New York,"
reading music from their iPads.

4

Now

a flower

made of flowerets—

a lantana—

is minding

the gaps

Moment to Moment

for Wallace Stevens

1

      Orange
poppy-speckled glass
vase alone

on a shelf,
neck twisted
to one side

like nothing else
in this guest room,

you organize
nothing.

2

      Overbearing,
that sleek leaf,

a yacht
on a stalk,

its long sharp prow
and curved gunwale
flanges,

the metaphorical
sum of itself.

Fusion

When we recognize we "think again"
without knowing what or if
we thought before.

I confuse copper
with brass.

To recognize is almost
always a pleasure;
perhaps it is pleasure itself.

I confuse Melissa
with Melissa.

To recognize is not
only to give something a name
but to give it the very name
that was waiting for it

somewhere

as if thing and name had been
sad without each other.

That's a woman
in an arctic fox costume
singing, "Don't you worry
'bout a thing,
baby."

I confuse worry with

~

Darkness in the shape
of leaves
flows over a building;

black ellipses
on the bay

slipping
and falling into place

Seams

A narcotic heaviness (lightness)
in which objects appear

to float or
seem to suffice

as is, as sleep
is no longer necessary,

no longer different
from waking.

It is here that gourds
fill to bursting

on either side
of seams. Here

words split
(multiply)

a long now
ago

Nothing

Excess has its own set
of sentiments.

For instance, there's a special
frisson you get
from squandering
in public
while remaining
nearly expressionless.

You could refer
to the undergarments
of Japanese schoolgirls
in passing
because why not
and because
you shouldn't.

Show us
you've got no skin
in the game
you've been playing
with yourself
for decades.

You are nothing
if not balanced
on the thin line
between class-system kitsch
and "That's all you got,
really?"

Distinguish

While you were out,
they built Kensington Commons.

You thought, "Princess-
sheep-Little-Bo-Peep-
ha-ha," but there was no room
left for such thoughts.

~

Would you like the ability
to add a location
to your tweets?

~

When you came to,
commons meant condos
and "distinguished living."

You said,
"My own being
grows faint
and fades away,"

said it
as if speech
prevented what is said
from taking place.

Then said it
amazed
that "own"
and "being"
could have been joined

in that way

Presents

Limpid green sea
laps the wall
of a ruined fortress
on a silent
television

until

a solitary
crooked pine
grows
between flat stones
at dawn

～

Complicated loves
are best—

and that things should change
but be equivalent.

～

Now I'm turning
tangles
into bows

on the present—
on each present
as it appears.

Can a bow
be bold
simply?

No.

A bow must
curl
back on itself.

Spun

As sadder than ever
may represent
the new
among today's
offerings.

~

As representation
is magical
spun straw.

~

After what passes for thought,
she leans forward,
extracts
a honey flavored
cough drop
from its yellow
packaging.

Traffic

The trees, good seraphim,
begin to sing

at dawn
about making sugar

out of light
and the happy traffic

between high and low—
as if that were all

~

I expect compensation
for all I don't
say—

for each time I stop
before coming

to an obvious conclusion
or an uncertain end—

for my discretion.

~

(Music needs silence
more than silence needs music.)

Negotiations

1

The best part
is when we're tired
of it all
in the same degree,

a fatigue we imagine
to be temporary,
and we lie near each other,
toes touching.

What's done is done,
we don't say,
to begin our transaction,

each letting go of something
without really
bringing it to mind

until we're lighter,
sicker,
older

and a current
runs between us
where our toes touch.

It feels unconditional.

2

Remember this, we don't say:

The Little Mermaid
was able to absorb
her tail,

refashion it
to form legs.

This meant that
everything's negotiable

and that everything is played out
in advance

in secret.

Refresh

Caterpillars munching leaves
(of the yellow-flowered cassia)
to threads
release this swirl
of yellow moths,
this August.

~

You are having "this experience,"
you say,

as if it pre-dated you.

(It did.)

~

You dream (always)
of rummaging,

no, sorting

through the contents
of a chest

as if there were
a best order

for these spun
shapes, colors,

ersatz heirlooms,

freshly re-
membered

Translations

Tissue thins
(with age)

to reveal
pale blue

morning.

∿

I keep making
these mistakes

because I know I'm wrong

                              somewhere

and I hope to be
misrecognized.

∿

As if on fire,
one eucalyptus

on the quiet
corporate campus

is flinging its limbs around

Signaling

"Keep it real" we say.

Thought is so distilled
there are punch lines
with no jokes attached.

~

It's complicated.

At the bottom
of the silver
wastebasket
at The Standard,
a boutique hotel,
is a round plaque
stamped
with this likeness:
an orange stick figure
vomiting
into an orange trash can.

~

And the small shrug
of a lone wave
in the shallows—

is romantic

Bees

If not being (something)
is the same as being,

then I will live forever.

~

Round shadow inside
the sunflower's

corona.

~

If I lived forever
would the present's noose

be looser?

~

Moon shadow
made of angry bees,

confined. Come in.

The Show

Silica bits
winking
in time's hardpack.

~

Ability to process
vast distance
at a glance.

~

Mortifying moment
that cost worker
big

~

What he confused
with transmission

~

Wiry, cloned
cages
throw black lines
on sand.

~

In the next round,
the surreal
is kitsch.

~

You call that vast?

Vessels

for H.D.

Hopeful vessels:
a few petals,

thrown up overnight,
fragile

amber flutes,
the sun's

grail cups
were not meant

〜

Beauty,
you've sexted me
too often.

Your pert leaves,
coming to a fine point
at the glass

stop at nothing

〜

If we hear
the same sequence

twice,

then someone's flaunting
"inner logic,"

but the wind loose
in copper chimes

is now far
more

The Act

1

Atoms are speech acts,
courting and shunning

like teenage girls
at recess,

exchanging zingers.

Sans organs,
they sense each other
at a distance.

So what are your chances
of finding peace
"within?"

2

Let's say your shtick
is to perform a version
of the trick you're dissing,
but so subtly
that no one notices
or, when they do, nobody knows
if you "meant it"
or what you could have
meant by it.

3

"Stay in the moment."
Find its contours,

like the walls
of your stomach,

that uniform sensation
of emptiness

experienced
as weight

Inner

Heaven, if it exists,
is when

there is no difference
between watching

and being watched.

~

"Show-off!"

~

Then quark and anti-quark
auto-correct

and I get
"glaze-hog"

for my inner
Santa

Object Lessons

1

That a memory,
caught and mounted

for permanent display,
is not much

like anything that happens
can't be surprising.

But where does that leave us?
Night at the Museum,

the set pieces
in their comic

ignorance of one another
take the stage.

2

In this series,
he tosses her

on the bed
like laundry

as she struggles
irrelevantly

against the stickiness
of tape

and it's just this:

the blind persistence
of her struggle

and his (feigned?)
indifference,

the way each proceeds,
blinkered and mechanical,

into whatever
this recreates

Normal

Intelligence is distributed.

Greed is an emergent property.

My survival instincts are a normal
form of momentum.

I don't feel bad
about crushing others
to achieve my goals.

Goals are an emergent property.

Others are distributed.

Hate

The market hates itself
just as much
as you hate it.

Look,
in this spread
for leather products,
a stern-faced man
in pink pants
and a bomber jacket
stands on satin sheets
in front of leopard print
wallpaper
holding a small briefcase
or purse.

The market hates you
even more
than you hate yourself.

Ahead

1

"Event-goers" herded
into "viewing pens"

(snipers on the roof)

to celebrate
"the safest New Year's ever."

~

"Personalities" paid
to count backwards
and kiss strangers.

2

Unruly and ruled
in shifts,

we've *tried*
to enjoy orbiting.

~

As if turning
off and on

was a sacrament—

the old sexy!

~

Patient
as grown women
in schoolgirl pleats

waiting for the
"headmaster"

Give Pause

Before we knew
what pleasure meant

we were multiplying,
going forth

into surrounding space
until all space

was pain.

~

Someone was mimicking
our squawks and jerks

as if they'd been
deliberate,

as if to say,
"Do that again!"

This was love, not mockery—
so we believed.

~

"What if someone saw you
in the tub," you teased,

as if my house, my head,
your head was crammed

with hostile relatives.

2

Let us give pause.

When one has
rippled
and recovered

the image
of the sky
again

one is
most

oneself?

Hence

Sculpted minarets
of clouds gone

hence—or thence?

No dreams
are that well formed.

~

No one can depict

the absolute bracelets
of the orbits

touched upon
by electrons

as feeling dithers
between words

Somewhere

If I look down, a ferry is always
docking or pulling away from the shore.
I am not always aware of these goings-on
any more than I am my own breathing,
but, when I do take note,
the sense of overseeing this step
in a process that's both
open-ended and fixed
fills me with a vague dread

while passengers,
whether boarding or landing,
may feel they are finally
getting somewhere

Judgment

Who are we to judge
the predilections
you cosset?

We will be discussing only
the difficulty
and expressiveness
of the gestures you use
to indicate them.

~

Is free fall
the opposite
of motion?

~

Funky Frogs
in the Adventure Aquarium
are "very relatable."

~

But bonus points are awarded
to those who indicate
a taste
for something not yet
conceivable:

Paper-thin girl
heading back to work
in a gingham miniskirt
shirtwaist dress
and ankle boots—

bingo!

Logistics

"Packet security."

He, she, they
were here to oversee
packet security.

It was the only
game in town

if this strip
of abandoned

staging areas
deserved the name

and no one
had checked recently.

What remained
to be demonstrated

in each
gesture toward narrative

was a tough-minded
nonchalance

we could almost
place

it was so retro
and thus plausibly—

or implausibly—
authentic,

but, in any case,
passing through

Flux

1

Come on poets,
word it

till it's yours
or no one's

the way the clock
on my nightstand,

long hand
bonking the numbers
feverishly,

is no one's

2

Sing Muse
of who's what
in this deluge.

The flux of dreaming
carries language with it.

A narrator
must stand aside
and mimic.

Where is he
when the whole worm
burns

from mouth to anus?

What is he
if the worm
refuses?

Cottage Industry

My long career
in explaining
my career,

my way
of proceeding,

my careen.

~

Single-car garage door
wreathed in puckered husks
of bougainvillea flowers.

Poem.

Empty street
above which

the invisible planes
roar.

Oh little!

Practice

1

In the future,
fewer people

"in your life,"

more in the world.
More strangers.

Practice being one.

This one
may meet your eye

if she thinks
you can help

or if she has forgotten
hope.

2

Bract

of euphorbia branches
through a window.

Days spent alone
with sight and sound,

the odd word

Trance

We know our dreams aren't real
because in dreams
there is no difference

between the will
and the unwilled.

~

And God divided "the"
from "the" and
placed an angel's
sword between
them and

~

We know the real
by its reluctance.

Still,

such inertia
looks a lot like
trance

It Is

"Is" concusses.

"Is" with its
orbital rings.

Heavy drops hitting
the surface
of a pond,

one after
one,

always.

The sweet voice
of its
hollow-bodied gong

left hanging

So

So that nothing
rhymes with much—

or starts to
and thinks better of it.

~

Ending with "like"
or "so."

Ending with "as if"

~

Virtual particles
carry the current

Acknowledgments

Thanks to the editors of the following magazines and anthologies:

Academy of American Poets' Poem-a-Day, *The American Journal of Poetry*, *American Poets*, *The American Reader*, *Barrelhouse*, *The Believer*, *Bennington Review*, *Black Tongue Review*, *Bomb*, *Boston Review*, *The Brooklyn Rail*, *Capilano Review*, *Colorado Review*, *Conjunctions*, *Cordite*, *The Economy*, *Epiphany*, *The Fiddlehead*, *Free Verse*, *Golden Handcuffs*, *Granta*, *Jacket2/ Poetry and Poetics*, *The Kenyon Review*, *Lana Turner*, Lit Hub, *The Nation*, *The New Republic*, *The New Yorker*, *Plume*, *Poetry*, *Prelude*, *A Public Space*, *Tin House*, The Volta

In the Shape of a Human Body I Am Visiting the Earth: Poems from Far and Wide (McSweeney's, 2017)
Plume Poetry Volume 5 (MadHat Press, 2017)
The PIP Anthology of Poetry of the 21st Century (Green Integer, 2016)

About the Author

Rae Armantrout has published fourteen books of poetry. Her books with Wesleyan University Press include *Veil* (2001), *Up to Speed* (2004), *Next Life* (2007), *Versed* (2009), *Money Shot* (2011), *Just Saying* (2013), *Itself* (2015), *Partly: New and Selected Poems* (2016), and the chapbook *Entanglements* (2017). She is professor emeritus in the literature department at University of California San Diego.

An online reader's companion is available at http://raearmantrout.site
.wesleyan.edu